Stop Sabotaging:

A 31 Day DBT Challenge To Change Your Life

By Debbie DeMarco Bennett

(aka Debbie Corso)

© 2012 and 2021 Debbie Corso (Debbie DeMarco Bennett)

This book is sold with the understanding that the writer is not engaged in providing psychological or other advice. Only a licensed psychiatric professional can provide a diagnosis and treatment information. If such services are needed, please contact a qualified professional.

Stop Sabotaging: A 31 Day DBT Challenge To Change Your Life is a work of nonfiction, but the writer has occasionally changed the names and other identifying information about places and persons in order to protect their privacy.

Clip Art Courtesy of: http://openclipart.org/

Photographs courtesy of the author unless where otherwise noted in References section.

All Rights Reserved

Table of Contents

Prologue

What is Sabotaging?

Some Borderline Issues That Lead to Sabotaging

Start of Daily DBT Challenge

Day 1: Self-Care Challenge

Day 2: Mindfulness and Self-Esteem Activity

Day 3: One Thing At A Time (One Mindfully)

Day 4: Identify Yourself

Day 5: Build Mastery

Day 6: Build Positive Experiences

Day 7: Be a DEAR

Day 8: Self Respect (FAST)

Day 9: Opposite Action

Day 10: Improve The Moment

Day 11: Work On A Relationship (GIVE)

Day 12: Think Dialectically

Day 13: Tapping Into Your Wise Mind

Day 14: Relax

Day 15: Contributing

Day 16: Pushing Away Thoughts

Day 17: Self Awareness

Day 18: Do Only What Is Needed

Day 19: Radical Acceptance

Day 20: Cope Ahead

Day 21: Crisis Survival Plan

Day 22: You Are Not Your Emotion

Day 23: Thoughts Are Just Thoughts

Day 24: Maybe It's Not All You

Day 25: Half Smile

Day 26: Self Love Collage

Day 27: The Electronic Break

Day 28: Practice Loving Kindness

Day 29: Re-Parenting Your Inner Child

Day 30: The Mindful Moment

Day 31: Set Your Intention

Wrap Up

References

About the Author

"If we have a part to play in the misery we're experiencing, this means that the power to change our circumstances -- our very lives -- is also within us. It's all about choices."

-Debbie DeMarco Bennett (Corso)

Prologue

Many of us with Borderline Personality Disorder (BPD) reach a point where we realize our lives have become unmanageable. We realize that the same old ways of reacting, responding, and behaving that we have held onto and practiced simply no longer serve us. They are in fact, sabotaging everything we hold dear.

If you are in this place, there is hope for you. I was once in your shoes. My life was a mess. I made the same mistakes over and over again, and I was desperate to figure out how to change. The problem that I faced, and that you have likely faced up until now, is that I had absolutely no idea where to begin.

In my first book, *Healing From Borderline Personality Disorder: My Journey Out Of Hell Through Dialectical Behavior Therapy*, I shared my documented experience of being diagnosed with BPD and my intensive two years in Dialectical Behavior Therapy (DBT), the treatment of choice for people with BPD. I was very pleased to find that in sharing my very private struggles publicly with others, many found or restored hope in their own ability to save and enjoy their own lives.

This book that you hold in your hands covers one of the questions I repeatedly received from readers hungry to take that first step toward healing and recovery: "How did you stop sabotaging your life?" And, more importantly, "How do *I* stop sabotaging my life?"

The fact that one would even ask this question is a hopeful sign. There has been a realization that things no longer work and that something must be done to bring healing to your emotionally wounded soul.

The first part of the answer is: We get to CHOOSE how we will respond when we are upset, emotional, and even when we are triggered. This is incredibly liberating and empowering when we truly "get it." I will, of course, elaborate as we move forward.

As you are learning this new information, taking it all in, processing it, and applying it, please keep in mind that you are not alone. As you read this book, think of the many others reading it alongside you around the world.

Think of the impact that willingly taking the time to work on your core issues will have on you as well as the ripple effects to those in your life and beyond. We cannot change without affecting others and our surroundings. Your decision to embark on a path of self-discovery and to do the tough work that comes along the way is a gift not only to yourself but to others as well. I personally wish everyone would choose to become introspective and work on being the best version of themselves. You're doing that.

I will walk you through examples of how sabotaging has manifested in mine and others' lives. You'll recognize yourself in some of the stories, and that's okay, because we will then explore specific strategies of how I and others have worked to repair and heal those broken parts of ourselves to contribute to becoming more integrated, emotionally healthier people.

Many of us with BPD did not have whole, integrated examples to model healthy behaviors for us. We can only learn by observing others' experiences and then choosing how to live our own lives. This does not mean we get to wallow in this or go on forever blaming others for our problems. At some point we must pick ourselves up and choose to take responsibility for the life we are creating going forward. DBT skills can help with this.

Dialectical Behavior Therapy (DBT) skills is a set of emotional skills created by Dr. Marsha Linehan that can be used to help people with a myriad of diagnoses. "Research shows that Dialectical Behavior Therapy strengthens a person's ability to handle distress without losing control or acting destructively" (McKay, Wood, and Brantley, 2007). Your author has recovered from Borderline Personality Disorder (BPD) and no longer meets the criteria. You will see mentions and references to BPD throughout the text.

These skills have profoundly changed my life, and I hope that you find your life enriched by them as well. Be sure to get a journal, as you will be writing as part of the challenge. Any old notebook will do, as will a memo app on your phone, but I recommend going and getting yourself a beautiful journal/diary/notebook. Pick something lovely and visually appealing -- something you'll look forward to sitting down with and writing. Perhaps, my *Self-Care and Emotion Regulation Inspirational Journal* will appeal to you.

I hope this book you hold in your hands serves as a source of hope, encouragement, and validation for you as you embark on this journey. I'm excited for you and the life you will create from this moment forward. Should you want to go deeper and study with me online, please visit www.emotionallysensitive.com for more information.

In kindness,

Debbie DeMarco Bennett

(aka Debbie Corso)

What is Sabotaging?

According to Google Dictionary, to sabotage means to: "[d]eliberately destroy, damage, or obstruct (something)…the action of sabotaging something" (Google, 2012).

sab·o·tage

verb / sabəˌtaZH/
sabotaged, past participle; sabotaged, past tense; sabotages, 3rd person singular present; sabotaging, present participle

1. Deliberately destroy, damage, or obstruct (something), esp. for political or military advantage

noun / sabəˌtaZH/

1. The action of sabotaging something

Let's read that definition again. Did you catch that? Sabotaging is a *deliberate* act of damaging, destroying, or obstructing something. When I came to realize that *I* was the one who was destroying my life, my jobs, and my relationships -- when I realized that *I* was the one adding to the damage -- that *I* was the one obstructing the goals I so deeply longed to achieve, I knew I had a choice.

I could either further victimize myself by falling into woe-is-me self-judging and self-damning thinking, ala "It's all my fault. I can't do anything right. I'm doomed," (which I did, initially,) or, I could cast aside the drama, move from Emotion Mind to Wise Mind, the place where we are able to rationalize, sort out thoughts, and make informed decisions, and realize the <u>gift</u> of that realization.

If we have a part to play in the misery we're experiencing, this means that the power to change our circumstances -- our very lives -- is *also* within us. It's all about choices.

The power is not in some other person or some other thing. Just as our thoughts, actions, and behaviors have been used as powerful negative influencers in our lives, they can also be used as powerful builders, reconstruct-ers, and healers in our lives. There's something very empowering about this.

A pivotal moment of this realization for me was early on in my diagnosis of Borderline Personality Disorder. I showed up at the crisis clinic, yet again in despair and inconsolable. I was buckled over crying and wailing. I felt so desperate, alone, and empty. I needed someone to help save me from myself. I needed someone to reassure me that I would be ok -- to comfort me.

My individual therapist happened to be working in the crisis office the day that I showed up, so I was able to sit down and speak with her. I'll never forget when she said to me: "All due respect, Debbie…what do you expect us to do for you?"

My initial visceral reaction was one of terror. What? You're not going to help me? I've burned this bridge? You're abandoning me? Rejecting me? I want to die! (Insert a flood of suicidal thoughts.) All of those thoughts raced through my head, and I felt like I had a ball of dough in the pit of my stomach, but I didn't say a word. I felt paralyzed. I just looked at my therapist's face, and it was undeniable to me from her expression that she was experiencing intense empathy for me in that moment.

I took some deep breaths, calmed down, and realized that she did not choose these words to hurt me but to help me. I said, "I don't know. You're right." We came up with a plan for my safety, and I went home. Her words stood with me: "What do you expect us to do for you?"

As I continued to contemplate this, I realized that even though I knew this on a rational level all along, that these people at the clinic are just human beings like me, I had very high expectations of them. I wanted them to fix to fix me. I wanted them to make me whole. They couldn't.

Sure, they work in psychology and are trained to help people like me deal with distress and process through the issues of life, but at the end of the day, they go home to their families and build their own lives. That's what I wasn't doing for myself.

I put all my stakes in my psychiatric care and thought that I could only feel well if reassured by a doctor or therapist. I thought that I wasn't whole, that I didn't have all of the pieces within myself, and that I had to constantly seek reassurance from outside of myself.

Remember, there's cause for everything. It this is sounding familiar to you, why would you suppose that is? We behave in accordance with what we have learned. It's important to remember that if certain things were lacking in our upbringing, it is likely those things were also lacking for our caregivers when they were children. They passed on what they learned. It's up to someone to break the cycle. Will it be you? Even if you do not have children or do not plan on having them, you can take care of *yourself* in the ways that you didn't get to experience as a child. There is actually a special challenge later on in the book to help build up your precious inner child.

If we were not encouraged to believe that we could comfort, soothe, reassure ourselves, and practice skills to tolerate distress rather than sabotaging, how could we possibly know what to do? Naturally we'd look outside of ourselves and overly depend on professionals to help us to feel okay.

If we don't believe that we have the power, by directing our behaviors in new ways, to prevent things from falling apart in our lives or to cope with the aftermath when they do, how would we know any better than to continue on with self-destructive, sabotaging ways?

The answer is we don't, and that's probably why you're reading this book. Not everyone will relate to their childhood being traumatic or lacking in modeling of emotional coping, but many will. No matter whether this is the case for you, perhaps you've realized that the way you've been doing things is no longer working, and you want to start making changes. Maybe I'm the first to tell you that the key to the door you are seeking is within you. You just have to believe it and be willing to use it. It takes courage and strength, and with time, you can learn to Stop Sabotaging.

BPD & Sabotaging

One of the greatest causes of human suffering is believing that we cannot tolerate being alone. For many people with BPD, feeling alone creates an incredible amount of distress and sorrow. Even the mere prospect of being alone can cause us to feel triggered.

This can be for a number of reasons. In my own personal experience, it has often been a combination of a deep, aching, empty feeling triggered by loneliness, and a frightening sensation of free floating. Without someone else around to guide and cue me -- without someone there who I could assess and read and determine how to please, I felt invisible. I felt like I was nothing. I had no anchor.

Throughout my longest-term relationship, my significant other often traveled to Europe both for business and to visit with his family. I remember the first time he left. I couldn't bear to watch him enter security at the airport. It was excruciating.

As he disappeared further and further into the distance behind the glass -- where I could no longer touch him, talk to him, or beg and plead to him not to leave me -- I felt as if I was losing a part of myself. I was terrified. I felt abandoned and empty. I didn't know how I could possibly live with him being so far away.

The pain and fright would become intolerable, and, not knowing what to do with my feelings or how to take care of myself -- not knowing how to cope with the thoughts and believing that I was in danger when I was really just hurting desperately, I made myself so sick that I needed to go to the emergency room. I sought out comfort and reassurance in the only way I knew how: reaching out to doctors who would *have* to take care of me.

Each time I showed up at the emergency room, I regressed emotionally to my late teens. When a doctor or nurse would ask my age, I would feel so embarrassed and vulnerable. I would want them to perceive me as younger and treat me as such. I wanted them to take care of me.

I had no knowing that I had the capability to survive the pain of the temporary situation. I had no knowledge of any skills I could use to cope with the intense emotions rather than giving in to impulses and recklessly and repeatedly sabotaging my life.

If you are in this place -- if you feel like even the notion of someone you love going away is simply unbearable, I was once where you are now. And, as impossible as it seems, you can, if you want it badly enough, learn ways to soothe yourself through the distress, to tolerate the intense emotions, and you can learn new ways of coping that don't make matters worse. If I could do it, coming from such a desperate and (what I thought) hopeless place, you can, too.

It doesn't happen overnight, and it doesn't happen without a lot of effort on your part. Equally important is that you seek and receive the support you need to conquer the demons that get between you and your ability to peacefully exist, even if you're on your own.

You may have noticed that I began this chapter by saying that our suffering is caused by "believing we cannot tolerate being alone." Before I started DBT, I didn't really slow down to evaluate my thoughts. I often took them at face value. Same thing with my feelings. For example, if I felt afraid, I determined I *must* be in danger. If I thought I should give up on something, I would tend to just give up on it.

And, if I thought I couldn't tolerate being on my own, even for short amounts of time, I believed it and did everything in my power to avoid the terror that being alone evoked.

The great news is, all thoughts and feelings are not facts. There are many instances where, by habit, a lack of knowing, or even fear, our thoughts are not in alignment with reality. When we can tap into our "Wise Mind," (Linehan, 1998) we can more rationally evaluate the truthfulness of a thought or feeling and then respond and behave in reaction to this interpretation, rather than our initial, impulsive reaction.

Additionally, people with BPD are often compared to chameleons. We often morph our personalities, mannerisms, and even our values to match whoever we are with in a given moment. I once shared with my DBT therapist that I had a great concern that should all of the people in my life convene with me in one room, I would completely lose it. Why? Because I was one way with my coworkers, another with my significant other, another with my family, etc.

Everyone adjusts their behavior for different social situations. It's normal to be more relaxed at home with your partner than you are with your boss. There are social norms and acceptable behaviors in different environments. This is expected of us. Where I have seen this taken to the next level within my diagnosis is that I have completely adjusted my sense of self depending on the company I was keeping.

Even my values changed. I came to learn that, up until recently, I didn't really have any steady values of my own. I would shift my viewpoints on religion, my sexual orientation, career goals -- majorly important parts of one's sense of self -- literally from one minute to the next based on who I was talking to.

If I felt very "Christian" and then found myself in a conversation with someone who was Buddhist, I'd shift and begin to openly admire the person and become beyond intrigued with learning their belief system. In order to please them and have them like me, I would latch onto their words and express how I shared their convictions -- only to shift to the next person's values and beliefs.

As insane as this may sound to someone who hasn't experienced it, until just before my diagnosis, this was a pretty normal way of life for me. I was a natural shape shifter. Even though I have found it very difficult to commit to and stay with jobs long-term, I would tend to ace all of my interviews and nearly always be offered the position I applied for.

I have been offered jobs for which I had absolutely no interest and hardly any experience. I would get to an interview, find out about the job, perhaps realize that it wasn't all that I thought it was going to be, but instead of conveying this, I would (at the time subconsciously) scan and assess my interviewer, the company, and what they were looking for, and then I *became* that person.

It may sound very manipulative to people who don't experience it firsthand, and I totally get why that would be. I can honestly say that until my final nervous breakdown that led to my diagnosis, the behavior was just so natural that I didn't even realize that I was doing anything "wrong" or unusual.

There are different theories about why people with BPD adapt this way. In my experience, I theorize that because I was brought up in a mostly invalidating home environment and had to quickly assess the mood and needs of my caregivers and morph accordingly to get my needs met and avoid abuse, I carried this "skill" into adulthood.

The good news is, no matter our upbringing or previous circumstances, we can now start learning the skills we need to stop sabotaging our lives.

This book can be a part of your very important journey. The fact that you have this book in your hands indicates that you're ready to try something new.

Let's get started.

> "Self-respect is the fruit of discipline; the sense of dignity grows with the ability to say no to oneself."
>
> - Abraham Joshua Heschel

Day 1

Self-Care Challenge

Often one of the most difficult things for someone with Borderline Personality Disorder to do is engage in self-care. Whether we feel unworthy, taking care of ourselves feels unfamiliar, or we just don't know where to start, the day has come to begin investing in taking care of you: body, mind, and spirit.

DBT acknowledges that we must take care of all parts of ourselves in order to feel whole, integrated, and balanced, as illustrated in the PLEASE skills in the Emotion Regulation module.

By practicing these skills, we reduce our emotional vulnerability:

1.) **Treat Physical Illness**: Is there anything you may need to see a doctor about? Schedule an appointment for that overdue exam or to have your physician take a look at a concern that's been bothering you. Be sure you're taking all of your medications as prescribed, and if you're having side effects or have questions about them, check in with the prescribing doctor for advice and guidance.

2.) **Balance Eating**: Often when we are stressed, we either over or under eat. Do your best today to eat regularly and healthfully and to stay hydrated. I can't tell you the number of times I've felt completely out of it due to not eating enough. Taking care by eating regularly helps us be less vulnerable to certain types of mood swings. It's also important to take care not to consume foods that will cause you to feel triggered or too emotional, such as caffeine. My anxiety levels have substantially dropped since I've nearly eliminated caffeine from my diet.

3.) **Avoid Mood-Altering Drugs**: It can be so tempting to take a substance that will alter our state of mind or numb us from the pain we are feeling, but doing so only causes more problems in the long run and upsets our equilibrium in the present. It is essential to avoid taking recreational drugs and drinking alcohol if we want to focus on regulating our emotional state.

4.) **Balance Sleep**: Often when we're stressed, as with eating, we'll either over or under do it. This can be a tricky one, as the ability to sleep enough to feel well and balanced may seem out of our reach. When I feel this way, I do my best to do relaxing things before bed time and allow plenty of time to fall asleep. If I wake up in the middle of the night, instead of staying in bed and allowing my mind to race, I get up and distract for a while and then go back to bed. If it's going on two nights of disrupted or deprived sleep, I contact my psychiatrist about temporarily getting on a sleep aid or using my anti-anxiety medication to help me sleep. We all know what a difference it makes to get a quality night's sleep. The other end of the spectrum is over sleeping, and I am all too familiar with this pattern. Sometimes getting into bed and resting is the best solution, but if we spend too much time in bed, we can feel groggy, overtired, and thus affect our moods adversely. I've also been told that it can be a way of feeding into depression. So, if the temptation to crawl into bed becomes more and more frequent, let your psychiatrist know.

5.) **Get Exercise**: We've all experienced this -- it feels so much more comforting to stay curled up on the couch than to put on our walking shoes and get outside and exercise. I experience this repeatedly. What I also experience is that, if I am able to push through, I feel SO much better both physically and mentally after the walk, yoga class, or aerobic dance session. Not only do I know that I am doing something good for my body by releasing stress chemicals and increasing "feel good" chemicals, I also get a sense of accomplishment and can better enjoy my lazy activities. You can start small and build up to 20 minutes, 3 times a week, or whatever regiment your physician says is appropriate for you. It really does make a difference.

How does practicing the PLEASE skills help us to Stop Sabotaging?

When we take care of our physical needs and health, we become less susceptible to the erratic, often dysregulated emotions that we can be vulnerable to when we are not. If we are feeling more balanced due to this self-care, we may experience less impulsive urges, reducing our possibilities of self-sabotage.

Mindfulness and Self-Esteem Activity

I recently attended an Intensive Outpatient Program (IOP), and one of the activities that we did in our Mindfulness group really impacted me and stood with me. I'm happy to share it with you in hopes that you'll also have a very positive experience.

The group therapist laid out a variety of stones and seashells that she had collected over the years. They were all unique in terms of color, texture, size, and shape. She asked each patient to go up to the table and select a rock or shell that spoke to them - meaning they were attracted to it in some way.

Each person brought their selection back to their seat and then did the following mindfulness activities. Before reading on, please select a rock, seashell, flower, or other object from nature and then return to participate in these activities. It won't take much time, and you may be surprised at how you feel after completing the exercise. Just walk outside and pick up a twig or a leaf if those are more readily available to you.

1.) Using your sense of vision, look at the object as if you are an alien from another planet, carefully examining this new thing for the very first time. Describe to yourself everything you see when you look at the object. Pause. Take a few deep breaths. Shift gears.

2.) Close your eyes, and using your sense of touch, feel the various surfaces of the object. Notice how the object feels in your hands as you allow your fingers to explore its surface. Describe the textures that you notice and any sensations you experience as a result of touching the object.

3.) Open your eyes and hold the object to your heart. According to the therapist who ran the group, although this may seem odd, she believes that every object in nature has its own resonance. This made me think of a lyric from the theme song from the Disney movie *Pocahontas*: "*Every rock and tree and creature has a life, has a spirit, has a name*" (Menken & Schwartz). If you don't feel comfortable with this philosophy, think about this piece of nature in a way that makes you feel comfortable as you hold it to your heart. Breathe deeply three times.

4.) Next, hold the object up to your ear. Imagine what words of wisdom this object from nature might have for you. As silly as it may seem, we often engaged in this type of wonderment and connection with nature when we were children. Try to tap into that or let your inner child do this part of the activity. What words of wisdom does your object have for you?

5.) The final part of the exercise was the most difficult for most. We were asked to go around in a circle and describe our object while using "I am" statements. I encourage you to try it.

Here is an image of the rock that I selected for the exercise. The camera just couldn't capture the brilliance of its facets and the way they reflected light, but here it is, along with some statements I (and others) came up with:

I am strong.

I have many different sides, and they all reflect light.

I have beauty.

I am rough in some places and smooth in others.

I have been through a lot, but I am not broken. I've survived.

I have changed with lots of pressure, but I am still here.

How does being mindful and building our self-esteem help us to Stop Sabotaging?

Practicing mindfulness has been a huge contributor to my ability to stop sabotaging my life. When we practice, we come into the present moment. We become in touch with what we think, how we feel, and what is actually happening right now. We don't get dragged back into the past and old wounds. We don't project into an imaginary future that doesn't even exist.

In practicing mindfulness, we also allow ourselves to put time and space - a pause - between any thoughts or urges we have and taking any action. Instead of jumping from a thought to an action, we pause in-between to allow ourselves the opportunity to slow down and think things through from a place of wisdom, rather than emotional reaction. Just slowing down in this mindful way can help prevent us from self-sabotaging.

Focusing on our self-esteem and building it up reminds us that we are worthy of so much more than we may have believed up until now. When we begin to believe that we are worthy, precious, and valuable, we are less apt to engage in destructive behaviors that hurt ourselves and sabotage the progress that we work so hard to achieve.

One Thing At A Time

We live in a culture where multitasking is valued and expected. You can answer the phone, type a letter, figure out these statistics, and stand on your head at the same time? You're hired!

Unfortunately, this mindset is hurting many of us. Studies, such as one conducted at Stanford University (Gorlick, 2009) show that multitaskers are actually less effective than those who focus on one project at a time.

This makes sense to me. I've personally noticed that if I am attempting to complete multiple tasks simultaneously, none of them actually gets done as best as they could if I focused on each individually.

I've actually stopped talking on the phone while in the grocery store. Aside from being less annoying to my fellow shoppers, I've noticed that the shopping experience is much less stressful when I go in. I end up successfully following my list (for the most part), and focus on getting the items I set out to buy.

Before, I'd get caught up in my phone conversation (though not really paying full attention to the other person), and I'd forget items, get the wrong things, or notice that my shopping trip was excessively long compared with how many items I actually purchased.

I thought I was accomplishing more by having a phone conversation and shopping at the same time, but I wasn't fully present for either and would end up stressed. When we do more than one thing at once, we are missing out on those moments in life. We are not paying attention.

I realize that there are some circumstances, such as a Mom who must watch her children while doing other tasks, for example, where multitasking is essential, but for the most part, we can consciously choose to do things one at a time (or consciously choose to multi-task when circumstances make it necessary.)

This next challenge is an opportunity to practice One Mindfulness by doing one thing at a time.

We are going to make and enjoy a cup of tea, but we're going to slow down the process drastically. Read this list over so you know what steps to take, and then begin, pausing to notice between each step.

1.) Select a tea that you would like to enjoy.

2.) Take the tea bag out of its container.

3.) Hold the tea bag up to your nose and slowly inhale, noticing the aroma.

4.) Select a mug and place it on a counter.

5.) Place the tea bag in the mug.

6.) Get your tea kettle.

7.) Turn on the faucet, and fill the tea kettle with enough water.

8.) Place the tea kettle on the stove.

9.) Turn on the heat under the kettle.

10.) While waiting for the water to be ready, sit down.

11.) When the water is ready, stand up.

12.) Walk over to the kettle.

13.) Remove the kettle from the heat.

14.) Pour water into your mug and over the tea bag.

15.) Place the kettle down.

16.) Watch the water begin to darken from the tea.

17.) Notice any aromas as the tea begins to steep.

18.) Sit down and let the tea bag steep for the desired amount of time.

19.) When the tea is done steeping, stand up.

20.) Walk over to the cup of tea.

21.) Remove the tea bag from the mug.

22.) Put the tea bag in the trash.

23.) Add sweetener or milk or whatever you like to add to your tea.

24.) Stir the tea.

25.) Lift up your mug.

26.) Notice how the warm or hot mug feels in your hands.

27.) Carry the mug to where you're sitting.

28.) Sit down.

29.) Lift the mug to your face and feel the warm steam.

30.) Notice the aroma.

31.) Put the tea down and let it cool for a while.

32.) Look at and observe the tea.

33.) When the tea has cooled down enough, take a small sip.

34.) Notice the temperature of the tea.

35.) Notice the flavor.

36.) Notice how you feel.

37.) Enjoy your tea, sip by sip, all the while noticing how the warmth of the cup feels.

I bet you never realized that having a cup of tea could be broken down into 37 steps! Look at how much we miss when we glaze over the details and do things in an automatic or autopilot way.

This exercise can also be done when taking a shower or bath by breaking down each step (opening the bathroom door, drawing the shower curtain, turning on the faucets, etc.)

How do you feel after completing this exercise? What did you notice about preparing and enjoying tea that you never did before (or had long forgotten?)

How does doing one thing at a time help us to Stop Sabotaging?

We are less likely to be overwhelmed when we are able to give our full attention to one task at a time. Feeling overwhelmed leads to emotional vulnerability, which can lead to sabotaging. By slowing ourselves down and being mindful, we reduce our vulnerability to overwhelm.

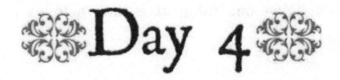

Identify Yourself

Not everyone has a strong sense of identity. This was actually one of the more frightening aspects of my condition that led me to receive a diagnosis of Borderline Personality Disorder. I didn't know who I was.

Does this sound familiar? Do your opinions, thoughts, viewpoints, and even values shift depending on whose company you're in? This was certainly my story.

The thought that led me to truly desire to develop a sense of my own, unique identity was that I wondered how I could possibly handle if everyone I knew where in the same room as me.

I was so different with different company, morphing into who I thought they wanted me to be in order to gain their love and acceptance that God forbid I should find myself in the room during a political discussion with a republican and democrat friend at the same time. Or a religious friend and an atheist friend. You get the point. This was a wakeup call for me.

I came to learn and realize that the development of my personality was stunted due to an invalidating home environment as a child. I was afraid of my father, so I'd behave in ways to try to desperately please him. I didn't understand my mother and feared her as well, so I'd act in another way with her. I had other mannerisms of behaving with each of my grandmothers.

Although, fortunately, none of these parts of me broke off into a separate identity or personality (as in Dissociative Identity Disorder, formerly Multiple Personality Disorder), I never formed a full personality of my own, and I carried the pattern of people reading and pleasing into my adult life. These behaviors served to help me survive as a child. They were my mind's way of adapting to my environment and protecting me, but as an adult, the patterns began to no longer serve me.

Figuring out who you are takes time, love, and self-compassion -- especially if, like me, you're getting a late start.

You may want to start out by listing some very basic things that you know or believe to be true about yourself. As you answer each question, patiently remind yourself to answer from your heart -- not what you think is the "right" answer, the answer your sister would give, the answer your father would want to hear, etc. Dig down deep. What are YOUR answers?

Pull out your journal and complete these sentences:

1.) My favorite color is _____.

2.) My favorite number is _____.

3.) If I could live anywhere in the world, it would be: _____ because _____

4.) The type of weather I prefer is _____.

5.) I feel good when I _____.

6.) The three world cuisines I enjoy the most are _____, _____, and _____.

7.) When it comes to cooking, I (choose one) usually enjoy doing it / do not usually enjoy doing it.

8.) One thing I know to be true about myself is _____.

Look at your answers. Review them while honestly assessing if the answers came from YOUR heart. I recommend making a note in your journal each time you notice something that you believe to be a truth about who you are.

Examples:

I love to get into conversations with others.

I am a vegetarian.

I prefer to wear comfortable clothes.

Keep a log and review it from time to time. Share it with your therapist as you continue to explore the unique, wonderful being that you are.

How does working on identity issues help us to Stop Sabotaging?

When we don't know who we are, there is a tendency to change course with every wind that blows. If we are not grounded in our own values and goals, we can easily become emotionally dysregulated and unbalanced.

Developing a clearer picture of who we are, what we stand for (and what we don't stand for) can help guide us in making decisions that lead us toward our goals rather than destroy our progress by sabotaging.

Build Mastery

When I first heard about the Build Mastery skill in DBT, I thought it would involve taking on an enormously challenging task and accomplishing it.

The good news is this skill only requires that you pick something to do that is at least somewhat challenging given where you are in your journey at the moment.

For one person, this could mean learning how to make fused jewelry in a one-day workshop. For another, it might mean finally getting the dishes washed and out of the sink. It really depends on how much energy you have on the day you practice and how ready and willing you are to push yourself.

Consider a task that you can complete today. Pick something that feels only slightly out of reach or challenging. It can be a housework task, an arts and crafts project that you saw online and have been meaning to try, a DBT homework assignment, or making an important phone call that you've been putting off. These are just examples. Think of your own life and pick one thing that you'd like to complete today.

Once you've completed it, you've practiced the skill of building mastery. Notice how you feel. Often times, we experience a sense of accomplishment and relief.

Begin a section in your journal where you log one task that you intend to practice each day, and then complete the task and log your accomplishments for the duration of the challenge (and beyond, if you find the practice is helping you on your journey.) Allow yourself to grow with increasingly challenging tasks as the month goes on.

How does building mastery help us to Stop Sabotaging?

We are often very hard on ourselves and don't keep track of all of the things we do *right*. By planning and documenting tasks that you complete successfully, you'll counteract the negative messages that say you're not getting anything done. When we feel more accomplished, we are more likely to continue behaving effectively rather than sabotaging our efforts.

Build Positive Experiences

This challenge involves coming up with a list of activities that make or might make you happy. You will begin by scheduling, at least a day in advance, one positive experience for the following day. The goal is to schedule several, if you can.

The more we fill our day with opportunities to feel good, our emotions will follow suit.

Here are some examples of positive experiences that you can schedule:

1.) Have a cup of coffee or tea at your favorite café before work

2.) Go to a fun exercise class.

3.) Sit outside and have your lunch in the sun.

4.) Go to a movie.

5.) Go for a walk.

6.) Spend time with a loved one.

7.) Curl up with a good book.

8.) Curl up with your favorite TV show or movie.

9.) Go out to eat.

10.) Go to a museum.

11.) Bring a sachet of your favorite tea bag to work and enjoy it at your desk.

12.) Light a scented candle and meditate.

13.) Do some stretching.

14.) Have a delicious dessert.

15.) Cuddle with a pet.

Log in your journal what you will do today and tomorrow to build one or more positive experiences into your day. Also log how you feel, having engaged in these positive activities. Start a section and continue this throughout the rest of the month (and beyond, if helpful).

How does building positive experiences help us to Stop Sabotaging?

We want to enjoy life. When we're feeling bad about ourselves and our circumstances, it can be really difficult to remember to take the time to engage in pleasurable activities - or to remember that we deserve to do so. This challenge will help you get back into the rhythm of planning and following through on doing things throughout the day that make you feel good and brighten your mood. When we are feeling happier and more optimistic, we are less likely to sabotage.

Day 7

Be A Dear

Relationships are an important part of life. For many of us with emotion regulation issues, they can also be super challenging and emotionally draining. We may have never learned how to have healthy relationships and are trying to figure it out now as adults.

In DBT, there are many skills under a module called Interpersonal Effectiveness. In dealing with others, you ask which of the following goals you wish to accomplish in a particular interpersonal interaction:

1.) Getting What You Want

2.) Keeping a Good Relationship

3.) Keeping Your Self-Respect

Often times, our goal is a combination of these. For this exercise, we will focus on getting what you want. Many of us feel that we don't deserve to get what we want or that we have to go about asking for what we want in unhealthy ways that served us in the past but no longer do. With the DEAR MAN skills, we learn to assertively, though gently, ask for what we need in a way that is healthy and kind to both ourselves and the other person.

D = Describe

E = Express

A = Assert

R = Reinforce

M= Mindful

A= Appear Confident

N= Negotiate

(Linehan, 1993).

On a small piece of paper, write down the breakdown of "Dear Man" as shown above. Carry it discreetly in your purse or pant pocket, and have it with you throughout the day.

As soon as you have an opportunity to practice the skillset, whether with a clerk in a store, your spouse, your child, etc., give it a try.

1.) Describe the situation in term of what you are hoping to achieve (unless it is somehow already obvious).

2.) Express your thoughts and how you feel about the situation.

3.) Clearly ask for what you want, and firmly but respectfully say no if you are being asked to do something you don't want to do.

4.) Reinforce your point of view by explaining what good or negative results will come from you not getting what you're asking for. For example, "If you assist me with this, I'll be able to pick up my children on time. If you don't, I'll be late to pick up my children, and they'll be frightened waiting for me." Also reinforce the positive results by thanking the person in advance, "I'll really appreciate your help with this. You have no idea what it means that I get this taken care of. Thank you."

5.) Focus on the outcome that you want.

6.) Stay mindful of being respectful to both yourself and the other person. Also, accept if it seems that the situation isn't going to go your way this time. You've done all of the right things to assert yourself in a healthy way.

7.) Appear Confident (no over-apologizing, for example).

8.) If things did not go as you hoped, see if there is a way to negotiate -- give up a little bit of what you sought to achieve if it will cause the other person to meet you part way.

Be PROUD of yourself! Asking for your needs to be met or telling someone that you can't do something that they want you to do might be very new experiences for you. Keep practicing, and remember to "be a dear" when you do.

How does being assertive in our relationships with others help us to Stop Sabotaging?

Boundaries are often a huge issue for those of us who suffer from emotion regulation issues. We may have never learned clear boundaries. We may have had our boundaries violated time and time again. From this perspective, it's easy to get comfortable in the victim role, because we so legitimately found ourselves there so many times in our lives.

We now have the choice to stand tall, take care of ourselves, and decide how we will let other people treat us. Learning and practicing assertive ways to communicate with those we relate to in life - from close family members to the cashier at the grocery store, we can avoid passive aggressive behaviors and bottling up our frustration or perception that we are being treated like a doormat.

We get to set limits, express our needs, and let people know our limits. This takes us to a place of empowerment. When we feel good about ourselves - that we've asked for what we've wanted while being respectful to both ourselves and the other party, we are less likely to feel self-destructive or sabotaging.

Day 8

Respect Yourself

Yesterday we practiced a relationship skill that focused on assertively attempting to get what we want or setting a limit around something we do not wish to do. Today's challenge is to keep our self-respect intact when interacting with others.

The acronym for this DBT skill set is FAST:

F = (be) Fair

A = (no) Apologies

S = Stick to values

T = (be) Truthful

(Linehan, 1993)

On a small piece of paper, write down the breakdown of "FAST" as shown above. Carry it discreetly in your purse or pant pocket, and have it with you throughout the day.

As soon as you have an opportunity to practice the skillset, give it a try.

1.) Use fairness in dealing with both yourself and the other person. No outlandish requests and no being hard on yourself for having needs and asking for them to be met.

2.) No over apologizing. You have a right to have your needs met. You don't need to apologize for this or for asking in the first place. There is no need to apologize for speaking your mind respectfully.

3.) If you are aware of any values you have around the situation at hand, respect those. If someone tries to get you to go against your values, let them know you will not.

4.) Stay in the truth. There is no need to behave like a victim who needs to be rescued, to lie, or to exaggerate to get your needs met. You'll respect yourself more if you avoid these behaviors and just stick to the truth.

How does respecting yourself help us to Stop Sabotaging?

We all know how it feels when we sell ourselves short, giving in to others' requests or viewpoints even when they go against what our gut tells us is the right thing. In doing this, we dishonor ourselves, which can lead to feelings of self-disgust, which can cause a whole spiral of emotions that can lead to sabotaging.

When we live in integrity, keeping our self-respect intact, we can avoid a while host of negative emotions toward ourselves, making us less like to engage in self-sabotaging behaviors. We end up caring more about our well-being and the outcome of our lives.

Day 9

Opposite Action

Sometimes we feel like lashing out. Sometimes we don't feel like following through on things that we know we really should. In times like these, the DBT skill of Opposite Action comes in handy and can help change the course of our experience for the better.

I'll give you an example. Perhaps you and your significant other have been getting on each other's nerves lately. Everything she does - from flossing her teeth to clicking too hard on the computer keys - has been irritating you.

You may have found that you're snapping at your partner, followed by some guilty feelings for behaving that way. With Opposite Action, we act in a way that is opposite to our emotional urge. In this case, the urge is to lash out. The opposite would be to show some kindness.

If you're irritated and the other person is also snapping at you, being kind may seem very counterintuitive. You don't have to go to an extreme and be phony with yourself or the other person. Just a little bit of kindness will do.

Here are some examples:

1.) Say, "Geez, we're both kind of irritable right now. I think we both need a hug." (Then offer one.)

2.) Surprises your partner by making her favorite meal.

3.) Offer a foot rub.

Notice how you feel and your partner's response when you shift gears and the course of the situation by practicing Opposite Action. Note this in your journal. If your partner is not receptive, just breathe, accept that you tried, and don't let it ruin your day.

How does practicing Opposite Action help us to Stop Sabotaging?

Opposite Action is most often recommended when our emotional impulse seems out of proportion to whatever has triggered the emotion. In these cases, using this skill helps keep us from making a situation worse and helps us regulate our emotions.

Sometimes our response may very well be in proportion to the trigger, but we still want to reduce the emotion by practicing Opposite Action. The same benefits arise: keeping us from making a situation worse and helping us regulate our emotions.

Improve The Moment

It's often amazing to me how taking the time to do very little things can improve my mood. Maybe that's why many of us don't bother to try them -- they may seem so small and insignificant that they would be a waste of our time. I've learned to try them. They help!

Improving The Moment is a skill that comes under the Distress Tolerance module in DBT. These are skills to use to help you cope with distress when you are in a crisis and there is nothing you can do at the moment to improve the actual situation that is upsetting you.

Because we acknowledge that we have no control over the external situation at hand, this challenge is not about trying to change the circumstance. Instead, we accept that the circumstance is what it is at present (which doesn't mean that we also approve or enjoy it, of course), but we work on improving the present moment to make it a bit more tolerable for us as we wait for the storm to pass.

Here is the acronym for this skill set:

I= Imagery

M= Meaning

P= Prayer

R= Relaxation

O= One thing in the moment

V= (a brief) Vacation

E= Encouragement

(Linehan, 1993)

Here are some examples of ways to improve the moment. Write down in your journal the ones that you are willing to try, and write down any that come to mind that aren't on this list.

Imagery - Do a guided imagery meditation, imagining a safe place that you can feel soothed and relaxed. There are many good CDs out there. You can also search for "guided meditation" or "guided imagery" online, including on YouTube. Kp.org/listen has podcasts that you can download or stream for free.

Meaning - Sometimes it's helpful to think about the purpose or value in what we are experiencing. This can be a difficult one to achieve while in the heat of the situation, but it is possible. Think about other difficult times or situations that have passed and from which you have emerged with strength and lessons learned. Think about any good that can come out of this situation.

Prayer - If you believe in a higher power or are willing to open up to the possibility of one, reach out to God, or even your own Wise Mind. Turn things over to your higher power, and reach out in prayer for support, guidance, and help letting go.

Relaxation - Let yourself relax! You may feel that you don't deserve it or that you won't be able to. The first thought is inaccurate, and the second thought remains to be challenged. Try a muscle tension and relaxation exercise (can be found on YouTube or at kp.org/listen as "Progressive Muscle Relaxation"), take a hot shower or bath using your favorite scented body washes and shampoo. Do some yoga or gentle stretching. Focus on slowing down your breathing and counting your breaths.

One thing in the moment - We practiced this skill in detail on Day 3. Refer back to it if needed. Remember: just this moment; just this breath. Worrying about things that *might* happen in the future will not help you now, nor will dwelling in the past. Get busy focusing on something in the here and now, and give it all of your attention.

Vacation - A brief vacation can refresh us. Sometimes a spontaneous overnight stay at a hotel by the ocean or a bed and breakfast can help break the monotony and improve our mood. If this is not possible, you can take an imaginary vacation using the guided meditations or guided imagery exercises mentioned earlier. You can also choose to turn off your cell phone and stay offline for a day, or take a drive to somewhere pretty.

Encouragement - Tell yourself affirming reminders that you are strong, you've survived other crises and came out fine, and you will get through this valley, too. Remind yourself that like everything else you've been through, this situation is temporary, and it will pass.

How does practicing Improve The Moment help us to Stop Sabotaging?

We may have come to believe that we deserve suffering. It's not true. When we begin to allow ourselves to have moments of feeling good, even amidst a storm, we send new messages to ourselves that we are worthy of happiness, feeling well, and taking good care of ourselves.

We don't have to suffer every moment of a crisis. We can deliberately and consciously engage in a moment here and a moment there of something that brings improvement to how we feel, despite our current circumstances, knowing that they will eventually pass.

This self-love and self-care helps us to improve our situation rather than making it worse by sabotaging.

Day 11

Work on a Relationship

There was a time when I had only one really strong relationship in my life. The truth is, I don't have many more than that currently. I have my significant other, a friend I know I can trust, and some family members I can call on for connection and support.

Years ago, I had lots of friends and a wide social circle, but (pre-diagnosis) I was often impulsive and so emotionally dysregulated that I would sabotage relationships with my behavior and found my circle becoming smaller and smaller.

I'd like to have more friendships again, but I'll admit, I have some anxiety about it. Am I ready? Will I respect the relationships and not sabotage them when I become dysregulated? Only time and deliberate attention and practice will tell. So, I practice this skill alongside you.

One of the skills in the Interpersonal Effectiveness module is Attending to Relationships.

According to Dr. Marsha Linehan, we should be careful to not let hurts and issues/problems build up and become overwhelming by holding them inside rather than expressing them and working them out, we should use the skills we are learning to nip potential problems in the bud, and end what we consider to be hopeless (unfixable) relationships (1993).

Are you harboring any resentment over things that have been happening in relationship that you value? Write about them in your journal. In your entry, note the items you are harboring as well as why you may be holding them. Next, write some pros and cons of sharing the information (in a respectful, calm, and caring way) with the other person. Next, write the pros and cons of not sharing the information. Share the information with your therapist if you think it may be helpful in your process.

How does working on relationships help us to Stop Sabotaging?

We are social animals. Although some people to prefer to keep to themselves more, most of us agree that our lives are enriched when we have others who care about us and vice versa. As we begin to reach out in trust and develop friendships and watch as we get better at maintaining relationships and giving as much as we expect to receive, we value these connections and are less likely to sabotage them as well as our progress.

Think Dialectically

Can you relate to having thoughts like this at the same time?

Example 1:

"I want to eat another piece of chocolate cake" and

"I don't want to gain more weight."

Example 2:

"I hate you" and

"I don't want you to leave me."

Sometimes we experience the struggle between one part of us having a desire or thought and another part of us experiencing the polar opposite desire or thought. This can be really distressing, and in that distress, it can become difficult to make a wise decision. We may see our options as severely limited to the two polar opposite, black or white options that are coming to mind at the moment.

Let this be a red flag to you. If you're having all-or-nothing thinking, say what one of my favorite life coaches, Iyanla Vanzant says, "Call a thing a thing, people!"

Say to yourself: "Okay, this is a red flag. I'm going into all-or-nothing, black or white thinking. Deep breaths. Let me sit down and try to find the shades of grey.

In your journal, either take an actual example from your life right now, or use one of the examples above. Write down the two extreme thoughts. For illustration purposes, I'll use example 1 from above.

Option 1: "I want to eat another piece of chocolate cake."

Option 2: "I don't want to gain more weight."

Thought: I'm only seeing two possibilities here. Acknowledge the red flag for black or white thinking.

Explore shades of grey:

1.) I don't have to eat another entire slice. I can have a sliver or a few bites.

2.) I won't necessarily gain weight by having a little bit more cake -- it depends on other factors throughout the day.

3.) I can choose another sweet that's a bit healthier instead of having more cake.

How does exploring our dialectical thinking help us to Stop Sabotaging?

When we think we only have only two, very extreme options, we can feel trapped and anxious. We may see either extreme as unappealing or overwhelming. When we begin to acknowledge that there are other possibilities between the two extremes, we see that we have options. We're not trapped between two extremes. We can compromise a little bit and find other options in the middle ground. When we feel less desperate in this way, we are less likely to sabotage.

Tapping Into Wise Mind

What is your Wise Mind?

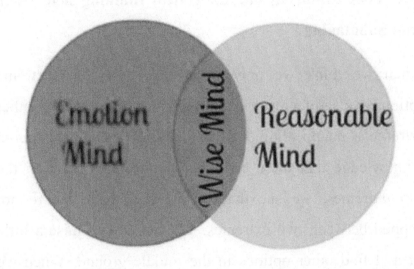

According to DBT, Wise Mind can be imagined as the intersection between our Emotional Mind and our Reasonable Mind (Linehan, 1993).

If we lived and reacted entirely from Emotion Mind, we'd be in trouble. We'd be behaving in emotional (and often dysregulated) ways. Emotion Mind does have its place. For example, we cry when we are sad. We feel angry when we've been wronged. We become compassionate when someone else is hurting.

We'd also be in trouble if we lived and reacted only from our Reasonable Mind. Whenever I think of Reasonable Mind, I think of the character "Data" on *Star Trek*. This creature, though he appears human, experiences no human emotions. He is only able to think in concrete, rational, factual terms. Reasonable mind comes in handy during activities like following a recipe, doing math problems, or other rational thinking.

Wise Mind, at the intersection, takes our emotional and rational thoughts into consideration and helps us find middle ground that will help us effectively cope with or get through a situation.

I had a chance to practice Wise Mind just today. I am feeling a bit under the weather with tummy trouble. Millions of people experience such symptoms on a daily basis. What complicates the situation for me is that I have a PTSD (Post Traumatic Stress Disorder) trigger around this particular type of physical ailment. When it happens, I often go into severe panic and anxiety and re-experience much of the fear and trauma from the incident when I was a young child.

I can tell you that I am quite pleasantly surprised about my ability to handle this situation this morning. The symptoms are the same as they have been in the past when I've reacted in extreme panic and terror, but I've chosen to stay in the present moment and use Wise Mind to stay calm and not make my situation worse. Here's what I've been doing:

Emotion mind, in an effort to protect me based on past experiences, is recalling a time in my life when similar symptoms affected me and I was alone and helpless. I am reminding myself, with Wise Mind thoughts and statements, that I am now 35 years old. I am safe. I know how to take care of myself. Although my symptoms are uncomfortable, I have the tools, insight, and knowledge to properly self-care and get through this.

Other things I've been telling myself:

Getting overly emotional will only fire off my nervous system even more, causing further upset to my body, including my digestive system. I know this from past experience.

I've been through this before, have used self-care, and have gotten better. This is no exception.

I can tolerate this temporary state of feeling uncomfortable, knowing that it will pass.

Get the idea? Draw the illustration of the Wise Mind intersection in your journal, and leave space on the rest of the page so that the next time you are caught up in Emotion Mind, you can come back to the page and start processing through your thoughts, like I just did, until you get to your Wise Mind. Share your discoveries with your therapist if you'd like.

How does engaging our Wise Mind help us to Stop Sabotaging?

When we act completely based on emotions or completely based on facts, we can make decisions that are unbalanced and not well thought out. When we allow ourselves to shift into Wise Mind and begin to come up with decisions from a place of wisdom, we honor ourselves and others around us. From this place of honor, mindfulness, and consideration, we are more likely to make helpful decisions rather than sabotage.

Day 14

Relax

I remember when I first started experiencing severe anxiety in my early 20s. If someone so much as, even with good intentions said "Relax," my anxiety would only escalate. Of course I *wanted* to relax, and if I could I would have been doing so instead of being in full fight-or-flight panic mode, right? On top of feeling panicky, I then felt the pressure to quickly feel better so as to not get on the nerves of the person in my company.

It can be especially hard to shift from a state of anxiety or stress into a state of relaxation, but with deliberate, conscious effort, it can be done. Many therapists also recommend having a regular relaxation practice each day. The thought behind this is if we regularly practice relaxation exercises, the state of relaxation will be easier to access and engage in during a time of crisis.

In your journal, list all of the safe behaviors that help you relax. Avoid listing things like alcohol or drugs.

For example:

1.) Curling up on the couch and watching TV

2.) Going to the beach and watching the ocean

3.) Taking a bubble bath

4.) Listening to soft, slow music

5.) Getting a massage

Choose five relaxing behaviors. At the top of your journal pages for the next five days, list one of the behaviors you will engage in to help you relax. On those days, write if you followed through. If you did, how did you feel before and after the activity? If not, use your Wise Mind to list what might have stood in the way of you practicing this challenge, and then give it another try for the next five days.

In addition, find a nervous system relaxation exercise that you like and begin practicing this daily. As previously mentioned you can find guided meditations or guided imagery exercises on YouTube or at kp.org/listen. You may find other resources by searching online or even in the CD section in the store (often under "Self Help" or "New Age").

The next time you feel panicky or anxious, pull out your journal. Write what the trigger was, then go and practice your nervous system relaxation exercise. Stick with it. If the urge to quit comes up, just say to yourself, "I notice the thought and urge to quit," and then let that thought go. Keep proceeding with the exercise. You are not at the mercy of that thought or urge. Thoughts and urges come, and they will pass if you don't feed into them or entertain them. Rather, stay focused on your goals. Allow relaxation exercises to become a daily part of your life.

How does practicing relaxation help us to Stop Sabotaging?

It's well known that our minds and bodies are intricately connected. It's also well known that anxiety and panic are responses that have long served to protect mankind from danger.

In today's world, we still experience the same types of reactions to fear and stress as our ancestors did, but very rarely are we actually in the same life threatening danger that they experienced. By calming down our nervous system, we send signals, or messages, to the brain that we are safe.

These messages are eventually received, and the anxiety and panic fades away.

Just slowing down our breathing sends a message. Tensing and releasing our muscles sends a message. The physiological benefits we receive when we are very calm during a guided meditation send messages.

When we are less in less operating from a place of fear and panic, we are less like likely to self-sabotage.

Day 15

Contributing

Sometimes, the best emotional medicine for ourselves when we're feeling badly is to do something kind for someone else. Not only do we make that other person feel better, but we feel better, too.

Contributing doesn't mean you have to make a long-term commitment to the local soup kitchen (though, if you think this is something you'd like to do, by all means, go for it!), and it can come in the form of the smallest of gestures.

How can you contribute today? Pick one or more items from the list below or come up with your own, and practice it. At the end of the day, write about it in your journal. Write about your deed, how the other person's life was brightened, and how it made you feel.

1.) Make a meal for a loved one who might be tired after a long day at work (or pick up the person's favorite take-out food).

2.) Smile at an elderly person and hold the door open for them.

3.) Let an anxious driver ahead of you if safe to do so.

4.) Surprise someone with a phone call, greeting card, or a craft that you make.

5.) Do someone else's chore for them.

6.) Stop to let pedestrians cross (it's the law in most states anyway!)

Contributing is a skill listed under the Distress Tolerance module of DBT. It is one of those crisis survival skills that you can engage in when there isn't anything else you can do to change your current situation, but you want to feel a bit better while you're going through the storm.

How does practicing contributing help us to Stop Sabotaging?

It's not easy when we are overwhelmed with our own emotions and circumstances to remember that the world continues to go on all around us. Others are also hurting or can use a helping hand.

For a moment, we forget our problems. For a moment, we remember that we can still do meaningful things, despite our own circumstances. The good feelings that result from both experiences can help us be less likely to sabotage.

Day 16

Pushing Thoughts Away

Most of the time in DBT, we are encouraged to accept and cope with our thoughts as they present themselves, but there are times where we should, consciously and mindfully, put thoughts on the shelf.

When should we do this? I'll give you an example of when I recently practiced this skill. Something terrible had happened to a friend's pet. The mere thought of the situation was agony for me emotionally. I'd burst into tears, feel so sad, and get angry. The fact was, there was nothing I could do to change what had happened, as upsetting as it was.

I had to let go of the thoughts, but it just wasn't easy to do.

I imagined the thought being put on a piece of paper and that I put the paper into a locked wooden box on the bookshelf. The truth of the thought still existed, but I needed to create a visual of pushing or putting it away and out of my immediate consciousness.

What good does it do us at all to relive traumatic thoughts during those times when we do have the capability to give ourselves relief in this way? Why should we continue suffering needlessly?

If you have PTSD or another condition that makes it seem impossible to push thoughts away, talk to your therapist about more advanced strategies.

How does consciously and mindfully pushing thoughts away help us to Stop Sabotaging?

In my personal experience, when I held on to reliving the traumatic incident that happened with my friend's pet, I kept getting myself emotionally and physically sick. I had to realize that as much as it hurt and as terrible as it was, no amount of reliving the scene in my head or getting sick over it was going to make the wrong right or undo what had happened.

I had to pull myself together, acknowledge the horror that I felt, and then imagine putting that thought away on the shelf and pushing it away. When it would try to creep up, I'd say to myself, "STOP" and quickly redirect my mind to another thought or activity.

Consciously and mindfully pushing thoughts away is a different process than flat out denying that something happened. You're not denying anything in this case. You are acknowledging what happened and your feelings around it and then giving yourself a much needed and deserved respite.

When we take care of ourselves by preventing re-victimization through thoughts, we are less likely to sabotage.

Self-Awareness

Without adjusting anything or moving an inch, notice your posture right now. Don't judge it as good or bad, just state the facts. For example, "I am slouching."

Notice the muscles in your shoulders. Are they raised and tense or low and relaxed?

How does your right foot feel? Is it all tensed up with curled toes or all comfy, relaxed, and warm inside a wooly sock?

On a scale of 0-10, with 0 being "the worst" and 10 being "never felt better," what is your mood? Just a number -- no judgment.

What you did by going through these questions was become self-aware. You noticed how you were sitting, your muscle tension levels, and your mood. Set an alarm on your smart phone, computer, or clock two times a day for the next five days. When the alarm goes off, note in your journal how you feel

- physically

- mentally

- spiritually

- energy level on a scale of 0-10

- anxiety level on a scale of 0-10

- joy or happiness level on a scale of 0-10

Consciously adjust once you become aware of what you're feeling so that you may feel even better in the next moment.

How does becoming self-aware help us to Stop Sabotaging?

All too often, we go about our days in autopilot mode. If we don't pay attention to our posture at the computer during the day, for example, muscle tension and pain may be building up and might lead to a headache that evening or the next day.

If we regularly check in with our bodies, we become aware of how we are and what we might adjust to make ourselves more comfortable. When we are feeling more aware of how we feel and implement ways to feel better, we are less likely to sabotage.

Day 18

Do Only What Is Needed

I'm writing this to you in the midst of a personal crisis. I still have them. I get emotionally dysregulated and distressed, especially when multiple, intense stressors happen at the same time. The difference between when I'd have these experiences in the past and when I have them now is that I work all of my skills so as to not sabotage or make the situation any worse than it already is. In the past, I didn't know any better. Sabotage was almost a knee jerk reaction to feeling overwhelmed with emotions and unbalanced mentally.

I think I was afraid that if people saw that I have a mental illness, that I'm not composed a hundred percent of the time, and that I have times of instability, I'd lose everything -- their friendship, my job - everything. I would catastrophize and then create the very situations I feared by acting out in destructive ways.

Now, when I'm feeling unbalanced, it's my red flag to practice doing *only* what is needed. What does this mean?

If you need to get through the day and leave the housework and leave the errands and only focus on those time sensitive things that will have consequences, then that's *all* you do. You take care of yourself. This might mean kindly and consciously breaking plans to be with or help someone else because you need some time to yourself.

It might mean just making sure you get out of bed a bit, stay hydrated and eat enough for the day. Depending on how intense the crisis is, you get to decide how much you can handle on a given day, and then *just* do that. It can help with recovery time significantly to take care of ourselves in this way.

How does doing only what is needed help us to Stop Sabotaging?

When we are in a vulnerable state of emotional dysregulation, it often doesn't take much to push us over the edge of feeling completely incapacitated by overwhelm. On days when our emotions are heightened and intense, if we take care to just do what is necessary, this is part of good self-care. We reaffirm that we need rest and to slow down.

We challenge thoughts that we have to be a superman or superwoman day in and day out with no break. When we take the time to slow down and allow ourselves some downtime and rest, we can prevent further vulnerability and not feel as compelled to engage in sabotaging behavior.

Day 19

Radical Acceptance

We all have those things in our lives that we just don't feel fully ready to accept. Maybe someone is ill. Maybe a relationship isn't working out as we had hoped and planned. It's as if we think that somehow, magically, if we don't acknowledge the situation for what it is, then it either doesn't exist or will go away. Because we are ultimately more rational than this, we always know that this issue exists in reality and in our consciousness. We are denying the truth of something rather than accepting it.

What is the reality that you are not accepting?

In her video series, *From Chaos to Freedom*, Dr. Marsha Linehan explains that Radical Acceptance involves the acknowledgement of the following three things:

1. Reality is what it is.

2. Everything has a cause.

3. Life can be worth living even when there's pain." (Behavioral Tech)

Let's take a look at these one at a time.

Reality is what it is. It doesn't get any more basic than this. The sun rises in the east and sets in the west. That's reality. If you preferred or wished that it happened some other way or denied that it happens the way it does, you're not accepting reality.

Everything has a cause. Sometimes we can trace a chain of events to figure out why something happened. For example, if you release an object from your hand and it falls to the floor, we can trace the cause to gravity. If you're crying and moody, you may be able to trace the cause back to a conversation you had earlier in the day. We can't always identify cause. The mind is so complex, and then there are times when there are physiological contributors as well. Whether we can identify the cause for our feelings or a situation, we can rest assured that there is cause. This confirms the old cliché that everything happens for a reason - the reason being a chain of events leading up to that very moment in time.

Life can be worth living even when there's pain. If we radically accept a painful situation for what it is, we can move on with finding ways to be content and possibly even happy despite our circumstances and without going into denial. We can find the happiness that exists despite the painful circumstances in our lives.

Is there something in your life that you are not accepting? This particular challenge is one that I find difficult and am continuing to work on. It involves identifying at least one thing in your life that you know you are not facing head on. In your journal, just for today, write what it is. If that's all you can do at the moment, just do that much.

For example:

My relationship with Jake is not what I pretend it to be.

Aunt Jan really is terminally ill.

Once you have written it down, consider talking about it with a therapist or someone you trust. How does denying the reality of what is at hand rob you from experiencing your life in the here and now? How does it take away from your closest, most important relationships? As you feel ready to explore these questions and work toward radical acceptance, jot down your answers and bring them with you to therapy.

Go easy on yourself. There are reasons or cause even for denying. Sometimes the truth of our reality is incredibly painful and we need to approach it slowly.

Another thing about Radical Acceptance is that, because it can be difficult to let the state of denial go, we usually have to repeatedly turn the mind back to acceptance. This means that when you notice yourself going back to denial, you take a deep breath and say something like, "I notice I'm resisting reality again. This situation may not be what I want, but it is what it should be based on everything that's happened up until now."

How does radically accepting reality help us to Stop Sabotaging?

I know someone who was in denial when her father was terminally ill in a hospice. He didn't have much time left to live. She was young, scared, and it horrified her to see her father in the frail condition she was in. To protect herself at the time, she went into denial about the severity of the issue and how little time her father still had to live. The result?

She missed out on spending quality time with him in the last days of his life. The reality is, she'll never get that back, and it's haunted her for a very long time. Of course now she must work on radically accepting the choices she made in the past and the reality of the consequences.

When we get better at accepting reality *during* difficult times, we can suffer less emotional consequences in the long run, which can reduce our tendency to sabotage.

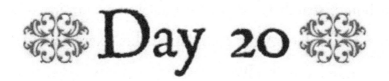

Coping Ahead

You know the feeling. You have an exam, test, work meeting, or doctor's appointment that you are dreading. Just the mere thought of it makes you panic. How in the world can you prepare yourself mentally to deal with the impending appointment while suffering as little as possible in the meantime?

Coping Ahead is a DBT skill that falls under the Emotion Regulation module. I've used it to prepare for everything from a work meeting to a legal session to a gynecological exam visit.

With this skill, you use your imagination to vividly think about the situation you are anticipating.

For example, let's say you have a written exam coming up. It would be ideal to know what the room looks like where the exam will take place. If it's possible to visit it ahead of time, this will help the exercise.

At home, search for a guided muscle tension and relaxation exercise online. After completing this exercise and feeling more relaxed both physically and mentally, close your eyes, and begin to think about the experience in advance. While you obviously cannot accurately predict everything that will happen, you'll use your imagination to guess. The preparation is a bit of an exposure exercise, allowing you to desensitize a bit to the fear around the upcoming event.

So, once your eyes are closed, imagine getting ready to leave the house. You grab your keys, head out the door, and get your car. Think about your route to the exam center. Think about the sights you'll pass, the time of day it will be when you're on the road, and imagine the scene as vividly as possible.

Next imagine arriving at the exam center. You park your car and head toward the building. Imagine all of the details of that walk from the car to the building. Look at the other cars. The sky. The sidewalk. Signs. Anything else you can think of. Add lots of detail, as much from the real scene as possible.

Next, take a few deep breaths as you imagine approaching the room, noting all of the details of the hallways and any other places you have to pass along the way. Imagine going into the room and sitting down to take your test. Take a few more deep breaths. Imagine receiving the test and feeling more relaxed than you ever thought you would. Imagine completing the test, handing it in, and feeling relieved as you leave the building to head home.

Try practicing this exercise with your own individual situation each day for as many days as possible leading up to the actual appointment. Notice if your anxiety level decreases as the appointment gets closer and, if so, how significantly.

How does Coping Ahead help us to Stop Sabotaging?

How many times have you ended up blowing off an important meeting or appointment because the anxiety was just too intense? I know I've cancelled medical appointments and even not shown up for interviews because I was so terrified of the experience.

I have missed out on many opportunities due to fear. What have you given up because the anticipatory anxiety got too intense? When our emotion of fear is dysregulated, it can be a hindrance, standing in the way of accomplishing things small and big.

When we cope ahead with potentially difficult situations, we provide our minds and nervous systems with a way to desensitize to the upcoming event a bit. We prepare ourselves for what to expect (as best as we can), and we take an edge off of the anticipatory anxiety. When we are less anxious about an important upcoming event, we are less likely to sabotage by blowing it off and missing out on important opportunities.

Crisis Survival Plan

You're working hard to free yourself from engaging in and resorting to self-sabotaging behaviors, especially in times of emotional distress. There may be times along the road, as I too continue to experience, when emotions become so dysregulated that you need to put in an extra amount of effort to keep from behaving in past, destructive ways.

One way to prepare for this is to create a Crisis Survival Plan kit right now, when you are feeling well enough to do so. It's important to create this plan in as clear a state of mind as possible and to be sure to refer to it should you ever need it.

On the very last page of your journal, where you can very easily find it, write at the top "Crisis Survival Plan," then write the following, filling in your answers according to your personal situation:

- A mental health professional I can call for support right now is (Name, phone number)

- A friend or loved one I can call for support right now is (Name, phone number)

- A crisis line I can call for support right now is (Name, phone number)

- I have been working hard to prevent myself from sabotaging, so no matter how bad this feels right now, I am going to focus on my short and long term goals and not sabotage. Some of my short and long term goals are (list them).

- When I feel distressed, engaging in the following activities help calm or distract me enough to let the wave pass: (list activities). No matter how bad it feels right now and how resistant or stubborn I may feel about taking care of myself in this way, in this moment, I am going to do one of these activities (then go do one).

Write in your journal about how you're feeling. What triggered it? What are the emotions coming up? What is the impulse? What skills are you using to choose healthier reactions rather than sabotaging? Be sure to journal after the storm passes to note your successes and challenges around effectively coping with the distress. Be sure to share your entire experience with your therapist.

How does creating and using a Crisis Survival Plan help us to Stop Sabotaging?

There are times when our emotions become overwhelming beyond our expectations. It's these moments when we need a plan to keep ourselves on track with our goals. Creating a plan when we are in a stable state of mind and able to focus on the reasons *why* we are working so hard will make the plan come in handy when those reasons seem elusive or distant. We can challenge our current state when in a crisis and remind ourselves to hold firm to our crisis plan, even when it may be very difficult. We can still do it. Having a way to cope during a crisis helps prevent us from sabotaging when emotions become very hard to handle.

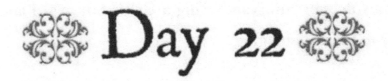

You Are Not Your Emotions

Think about the sentence "I am sad." Are you really sadness, or do you sometimes temporarily *experience* sadness?

In some other cultures, the proper structure of the sentence is "I have sadness." I think this is more accurate. After all, we are not our emotions. Emotions are transient states that we experience, and they come and go.

The next time you experience an emotion, especially a challenging one, try to separate who you are from the emotion you are experiencing by saying:

Instead of "I am angry." >> "Anger is coming up within me, and it will pass."

Instead of "I am anxious." >> Anxiety is arising within me. It will pass."

Remind yourself: "I am not my emotion. I am experiencing the emotion of (....), and it will pass."

How does acknowledging that we are not our emotions help us to Stop Sabotaging?

Emotions are powerful. I've found that if I over-identify with an emotion by saying that I *am* that emotion, it seems to linger longer. I'm not always conscious of this. Whether expressing myself verbally or in writing, I often say things like, "I am anxious." It's something I'm working on alongside you, because the longer an uncomfortable emotion lingers, the more distressed I get. If we can reduce our distress, we are less likely to sabotage.

Day 23

Thoughts Are Just Thoughts

The reasoning behind today's challenge is very similar to yesterday's. Yesterday we acknowledged that we are not our emotions. Today, we focus on how we are not our thoughts. Not only that, but we focus on how thoughts are *just* thoughts.

Here's an example. Think of someone who you love -- someone who is a kind, compassion, caring person. The person comes to you, upset over something that happened earlier in the day. She has a thought, and she expresses it to you as "I am so stupid. I can't do anything right."

Right away, you want to put your arms around this person, because she is clearly beating herself up emotionally. She does so many things right, and she is very far from stupid. She is having *thoughts* that she is stupid and can't do anything right, but these thoughts, very obviously to you, do not reflect reality. They are distorted thoughts during a time of emotional upset.

The same goes for our thoughts. Not all thoughts are facts. Sometimes thoughts are just thoughts. They come and go, and they are not who we are.

Today in your journal, note some thoughts that you were conscious of and that you were able to challenge. Pay special attention to thoughts that are negative toward yourself and others. Also write down what your challenge to each thought was.

For example: "This driver in front of me is an idiot for going so slow."

Challenging thought: "I'm angry right now because I'm in a hurry and this person in front of me is driving so slowly. They may have a medical issue going on or be frightened navigating a new road. I can take some deep breaths and let this thought go."

When you challenge your thoughts, strip them just to the facts. In the case of the example, the facts are:

1.) I'm in a hurry

2.) The person in front of me is driving slowly

3.) I'm feeling distressed in response to their slow driving

Not a fact: The person is an idiot.

How does acknowledging that our thoughts are just thoughts help us to Stop Sabotaging?

Once we learn that thoughts are just thoughts, they have a lot less power over us. I used to get the thought, "I have to get out of here now" when I was anxious, and I'd immediately leave the situation. When I began to watch my thoughts, I'd notice the fear and then say, "I'm having the thought that I need to get out of here now, but I don't have to respond or react to it."

I was so amazed by the innate power I'd had all along to be able to notice a thought but not be required to follow through on any part of it. When we realize that we have a choice about how we view and respond to thoughts, we are less likely to sabotage. We know we that we have choices and that we aren't compelled or controlled by our thoughts.

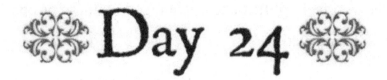

Maybe It's Not All You

I apologize in advance if I offend you with the vulgarity (one curse word) in this next example, but it so keenly captures the essence of this challenge that I had to share it with you. I saw this quote going around on Facebook recently:

> *"Before you diagnose yourself with depression or low self-esteem, first make sure that you are not, in fact, just surrounding yourself with assholes."* - William Gibson

I hope you had a little chuckle over that. Environmental factors like the company we keep, including the attitudes and behaviors of others around us and the types of places we spend our time, all affect our moods and emotions.

Think about the places where and the people with whom you tend to spend a lot of time. Write them down in your journal, along with the answers to the following questions:

- Do you feel uplifted and encouraged by these or oppressed and discouraged?

- What choices can you make about the places you spend your time and the relationships you're in with others?

How does acknowledging how our environment affects us help us to Stop Sabotaging?

When we realize that our environment can affect our moods and emotions, we can become more conscious about the choices we make with our time. We can consider whether a certain place is really all that good for our emotional well-being. We can think about whether our relationships are healthy and encouraging us to grow. When we realize we have control over making such adjustments, we see ourselves less as victims of circumstances. When we feel empowered rather than victimized, we are less likely to sabotage.

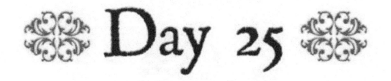

Half Smile

The fascinating thing about the connection between our facial expressions and our moods is that the communication is a two-way street. So, while we may experience an emotion and then have a corresponding facial expression, we can also reverse this process. By deliberately creating a facial expression, we actually send feedback to the brain that affects our moods.

The DBT skill for this challenge is called the "Half Smile," a genuine, semi-smile that we will deliberately do in order to have a positive effect on our moods. It's just a slight, up-curling of the lips while the rest of the face relaxes. It's not forced or overdone.

Look at this image of the famous Mona Lisa portrait. Look at her expression. This is a great example of the Half Smile.

The next time you are feeling melancholy, give this a try. I felt extremely silly the first couple of times I tried it, but when I saw the result I hoped for -- a shift in mood to one that was more positive -- I felt much less silly.

Practice right now, and document in your journal how you feel afterward. Think of it as an opportunity to practice Opposite Action to frowning.

How does acknowledging how our environment affects us help us to Stop Sabotaging?

Half Smiling is a tool that we can take with us no matter where we are. If we are experiencing a sense of melancholy and we'd like to shift our mood, we can discreetly and easily practice this skill. Witnessing how powerful our choice of facial expression can be on how we feel empowers us. When we realize we have a tool to help shift our mood for the better, even a little bit, we are less likely to sabotage

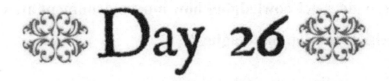

Day 26

Self-Love Collage

Today's challenge is a bit artsy to change up the routine. Whether you're a craftinista or you can barely draw a straight line - don't worry. This collage is more about content and less about presentation. Your self-love collage will be something for you to refer to, so take your time with it, be thoughtful and patient, and create something that you'll want to hold onto and look at.

What you'll need:

- a piece of hard cardboard or piece of construction paper. If all else fails, a plain piece of white paper will work, too.

- a pair of scissors

- glue

- magazines, newspapers, and you can also access the internet to print images from there

- markers, colored pencils, or pens

Find some time when you won't be disturbed for at least an hour. Perhaps put on some tea. Turn on some soothing music, and gather your supplies. Sit in a comfortable chair or on the floor, and begin flipping through the magazines and newspapers.

When you find images that call to you, cut them out and place them on the table or floor in front of you. Collect images that make you smile, images that represent something you hope to have in your life, images that evoke positive memories, and any other types of images you would like to include.

Cut out an image that, to you, says "Self Love." Paste that image in the middle of the piece of construction paper. Surround this with the other images you selected by gluing them on the paper. Decorate around the pictures or add words using your writing utensils. On the back of the paper, write today's date.

Save this collage and reflect on it over the next few days. Save it to reflect on it in the future.

How does engaging in an activity like this help us to Stop Sabotaging?

You've just engaged in a self-care exercise designed to give you some time to unwind and reflect. Were you mindful during this exercise? Did you find it to be a nice, even if brief, distraction from your troubles? When we take time out to be more relaxed and considerate of ourselves and we focus on those things that make us feel good - in this case represented by images - we are less likely to sabotage.

Day 27

The Electronic Break

In your journal today, write down all of the ways that you are electronically connected at this time in your life. Your list may look something like this:

- Cell phone

- Social Media

- Online Radio

- Email

Write down what you anticipate you would feel if you took a twelve-hour break from all of the activities on your list. Include how it would feel to take a break from those items that you may not be able to realistically take a break from due to, perhaps, work requirements.

Look at your list again. Which items, even if you do not want to, can you technically go without for a twelve hour period? Pick one or more of the items and plan to unplug for tomorrow. If you give up email, no checking or sending any emails during the break. If you give up your cell phone, no receiving calls, placing calls, checking voice mails, texting, or using your phone to get online.

Throughout the day, you may notice a bit of anxiety in response to the absence of this device or method of communication. Just notice it. Notice that you don't have to do anything in response. Distract and/or self-soothe until the feeling passes.

At the end of the day, write about your experience. Were you able to follow through? Were you able to keep the twelve hour commitment? What did you learn from this experience? What stood in the way or made it especially challenging?

How does engaging in an activity like this help us to Stop Sabotaging?

We often think that we are at the mercy of our urges, feelings, and thoughts. With this exercise, we can notice and experience the urge to quit and not quit at all. Exercises like this can build our confidence around our willpower and ability to follow through. When we feel more confident in these areas, we are less likely to sabotage.

Day 28

Practice Loving Kindness

DBT takes a lot of cues from Buddhism - especially around mindfulness practices. This next challenge includes a traditional Buddhist prayer. If you feel open and willing, follow along. If you don't feel comfortable, substitute with a prayer about kindness from your personal belief system, or write a few lines in your journal about what kindness to self and others looks like to you.

Today's challenge is to do something kind for yourself and three kind things for others. These things do not have to be big. You can smile at a senior citizen in the grocery store, hold a door open for a mother with children, or call someone to cheer them up. You get to decide.

Here's the Buddhist Loving Kindness Prayer that may help you get primed for action:

May I be at peace.

May my heart remain open.

May I realize the beauty of my own true nature.

May I be healed.

May I be a source of healing for this world.

May you be at peace.

May your heart remain open.

May you realize the beauty of your own true nature.

May you be healed.

May you be a source of healing for this world.

Tonight, write in your journal about your one act of kindness to yourself and three acts of kindness to others. Not how engaging in loving kindness made you feel and what it brought up for you.

How does engaging in loving kindness help us to Stop Sabotaging?

You've come so far on this 31 Day Challenge journey that I trust you'll be able to take this activity one step further. Part two of today's challenge is for you to connect with your heart and write a bit in your journal about how *you* think practicing loving kindness can help you to stop sabotaging.

Day 29

Re-Parent Your Inner Child

There are many people in this world who have a wounded inner child. Are you one of them? If you don't feel you are, write in your journal today about this fortunate aspect of your life and why you are grateful for it.

If you feel that your inner child needs a lot of healing, think about ways that you can begin to validate her or him and consider ways that you can begin to give yourself those things you longed for but didn't fully receive when you needed them.

Here are some ways that you can re-parent your inner child by honoring him or her:

- **Acknowledge and attend to your needs:** If you're hungry, eat. If you're sleepy, sleep. If you need a rest, take a nap. If you need a time-out, take it.

- **Allow yourself to play**: There is no rule that says that now that you're an adult, life must be constant work. Although your idea of fun may have changed from your finger painting days, consider sitting down and doing a simple, childlike activity like finger painting, playing with clay, or even coloring. One way to feel less awkward is to do an activity like this with a child. Your children (or nieces/nephews, a child you babysit) will no doubt have fun and enjoy the attention and fun activity, and you'll get to do the same right alongside her. Even if you don't have anyone alongside you, the experience can still be very rewarding. Allow yourself to be free and really get into the activity.

- **Reassure Your Inner Child:** The next time you're feeling emotionally triggered, remind your inner child that you are safe now. Do some grounding exercises to remind her what year it is, where you are, and how the past is the past. You will not let her be harmed in the here and now. Practice some mindfulness exercises to reassure her, or engage in some distracting and self-soothing activities to comfort her.

- Radically Accept the Childhood That You Actually Had: We can't change the past. As difficult as it may be to accept, what happened to us as children has happened. There's no way to undo it. There's no way to change it. There's no way to wish it away. It's important to remember that *accepting* the past is very different from *approving* of it. Do you approve of past abuse you experienced? Of course not. Do you approve of being treated badly or not having your needs met? Again, of course not. With Radical Acceptance of your childhood, you:

* Accept that what happened has happened, and there's no way to change it

* Accept that the people who were your caretakers were doing the best they could where they were on their particular journey. (Some may find this one debatable, but if I look at times in my life when I have fallen short of being in integrity with others and treating them with respect, I am open to the possibility that while I could have done better, I truly didn't know how at the time. Perhaps the same was true of our caregivers).

* Accept that there are things we can do now to help heal the wounds of our inner children, but they will take work, commitment, and time

- Work on forgiving those who harmed you as a child: This has to be one of the most challenging aspects of healing, and it certainly isn't something that you'll accomplish in one day. This is an ongoing process that requires lots of strength, determination, compassion, and willingness. It is something I continue to work on, and I still have a long way to go.

Just for today, absorb what you've read in this challenge. Write down any thoughts in your journal. As you begin to notice moments of opportunities to work on healing your inner child, note them in your journal. Also note any times you followed through as well as times that you didn't. Consider and note what got in the way. Have compassion and patience with yourself, as this is an ongoing, challenging process.

How does re-parenting our inner child help us to Stop Sabotaging?

Re-parenting our inner child is not an actual DBT skill. It is a process that can be worked on using multiple DBT skills. You may have noticed the following skills in use during this challenge: Radical Acceptance, Self-Soothing, Distracting, and PLEASE skills. When we find ways to work our skills into practical exercises for personal growth and healing, we are less likely to sabotage.

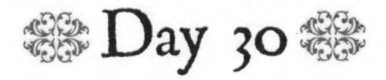

Day 30

The Mindful Moment

You've probably learned by now that being mindful allows us to slow down our thought and action process. It helps us to put time and space between our initial thought, feeling or impulse and any subsequent action we might take.

For today's challenge, when you get the urge to do something, take a few moments before acting. Start by noticing the urge. Stop, consider the short and long-term effects of any action you're considering taking, and then decide if the potential result of your action is in alignment with:

- Who you want to be as a person

- Your integrity

- Your short term goals

- Your long term goals

I used to have a real issue with sending impulsive emails, and it got me in to trouble on more than one occasion. I would receive an email, feel insulted, attacked, or otherwise be upset by it, and I would instantly reply. This would often result in embarrassing situations, especially at work. I felt like I couldn't control my knee-jerk reaction to messages that I interpreted as triggering. I would write back immediately with sarcastic, counterattacks.

It was such an eye opening experience to begin practicing the Mindful Moment. It took a lot of practice, but now when I receive an email that triggers me and notice the urge to respond quickly, I take that moment. As a result, I've saved myself so much unnecessary suffering, embarrassment, explaining, and apologies.

In your journal, write down some situations where you tend to have a knee-jerk reaction like I have had with emails. Next, write out a short plan on how you will handle the intensity of the elicited emotion the next time you are faced with that situation, and answer how your new response will fit in with the bulleted list of four items at the top of this page.

How does slowing down and being mindful help us to Stop Sabotaging?

Given how far you've come in your practice, this challenge continues. Write in your journal the answer to this question.

Set Your Intention

Congratulations -- you've reached the end of the challenge! You should truly be very proud of yourself. Sticking with anything for a month takes willpower, and considering the content and nature of this challenge, it also took a lot of strength and honest introspection.

The journey does not have to end here. You can continue to practice DBT skills every day. You can subscribe to Amanda Smith's *My Dialectical Life*, a daily DBT skill via email. You can read other books on the skills and search online for other resources.

You've started a healthy habit that you can continue to feed and cultivate.

In your journal tonight, write about your experience with this challenge:

- What did you get out of it?

- What is your favorite DBT skill?

- Which skills do you feel you need to practice more?

- What ways will you continue to practice?

- Will you continue journaling each day?

- Will you pick up books on DBT?

- Will you join *My Dialectical Life*?

- Will you look for and sign up for DBT classes in your area?

- How else will you continue on this journey you've started?

Setting an intention is a lot like setting a goal. In clear, specific language, write out how you plan to continue on this path, and refer to it whenever you need to.

It's been my pleasure to accompany you on this challenge.

Well done.

Wrap Up

Congratulations!

You've just finished reading a fabulous book by my friend, Debbie.

And now comes the hard part. This book just can't remain on your virtual shelf. You actually have to use the ideas and suggestions Debbie talks about—and you'll need to use them (or parts of them) every day for the rest of your life.

If that sounds like a supernatural challenge, that's because it's close to being just that.

Creating a life worth living may be the most difficult work that you'll ever do. There will be some days that you won't feel up to the task but if you keep moving forward this will become easier. In the end, though, success can be yours and we'll have been cheerleading you all the way.

You'll find moments of joy, meaning, and love. You'll be able to succeed at doing thing you would have never dreamed. You'll create and be an integral part of healthy and sustaining relationships.

This journey takes bravery and you are incredibly brave.

You can do this.

Dialectically yours,

Amanda Smith, LCSW

Amanda Smith is the founder of My Dialectical Life, which provides Daily DBT Tips and information via email. Make your DBT practice a daily practice that you stick with. Sign up for MDL!

About the Author

Debbie DeMarco Bennett (aka Debbie Corso) is a mental health blogging pioneer, courageously chronicling her journey while lighting a torch to provide hope to a severely emotionally wounded community. She has a Bachelor's Degree from New York Institute of Technology in Interdisciplinary Studies in English, Communications, and Behavioral Science and a certificate in Early Childhood Development. She is also a certified life coach and was trained in DBT Skills teaching through Dr. Marsha Linehan's Behavioral Tech institute.

Her first book, _Healing From Borderline Personality Disorder: My Journey Out of Hell Through Dialectical Behavior Therapy_ chronicles her journey from diagnosis through two years of

DBT and beyond, and she teaches DBT skills to people around the globe at www.emotionallysensitive.com

Her work as an Intake Coordinator and Case Manager at a non-profit organization, working closely with children at risk for abuse and neglect, was the catalyst that propelled her to document and share her powerful journey through her blog and now this book. She lives in sunny Northern California with her husband and two fur babies.

###

References

American Psychological Association (APA). (2012, November 9). *DSM-5 development: Borderline personality disorder*. Retrieved from http://www.dsm5.org/ProposedRevisions/Pages/proposedrevision.aspx?rid=17

Behavioral Tech. (Producer) (unknown). *From chaos to freedom* [VHS].

Corso, D. (2012). *Healing from borderline personality disorder: My journey out of hell through dialectical behavior therapy*. San Francisco: Kindle.

dpaint. (Photographer) (2009). *Beautiful girl playing with colors* [WebPrint]. Available from http://www.istockphoto.com/stock-photo-9378286-beautiful-girl-playing-with-colors.php

du Louvre, M. (Photographer). (2007). *The Mona Lisa (by Leonardo da Vinci)*. [Print Photo]. Retrieved from http://en.wikipedia.org/wiki/File:Mona_Lisa.jpg

Google. (2012, November 9). *Define sabotage*. Retrieved from https://www.google.com/search?q=define sabotaging&oq=define sabotaging&sugexp=chrome,mod=0&sourceid=chrome&ie=UTF-8

Gorlick, A. (2009, August 24). Media multitaskers pay mental price, Stanford study shows. *Stanford News*. Retrieved from http://news.stanford.edu/news/2009/august24/multitask-research-study-082409.html

Linehan, M. (1993). *Skills training manual for treating borderline personality disorder*. (1st ed.). The Guilford Press.

McKay, M., Wood, J. C., & Brantley, J. (2007). *The dialectical behavior therapy skills workbook: Practical DBT exercises for learning mindfulness, interpersonal effectiveness, emotion regulation, and distress tolerance*. New Harbinger Publications.

Mendhak. (Photographer). (2009). *Black tea pot*. [Web Photo]. Retrieved from http://commons.wikimedia.org/wiki/File:Black_Tea_Pot.jpg

Menken & Schwartz. "Colors of the Wind." Lyrics. Perf. Vanessa Williams. Pocahontas. Walt Disney. 1995.

Sankari1. (Photographer). (2012). *Rocks from coastal area north Norway*. [Web Photo]. Retrieved from http://commons.wikimedia.org/wiki/File:Coastal-rocks.jpg

Unknown. (Photographer). (PD-1923). *Paintings of Buddha meditating*. [Web Photo]. Retrieved from http://commons.wikimedia.org/wiki/File:Buddha_meditating.jpg

Made in the USA
Monee, IL
02 August 2025